Keto Ice Cream Cookbook

Table of Contents

Table of Contents 2

Disclaimer 7

Introduction 8

Keto Ice Cream Recipes 12

    Pumpkin Spiced Pecan Pie Ice Cream 12

    Chocolate Therapy 14

    Snow White Vanilla 16

    Lemon Ice Cream 18

    Sky Cheese Ice Cream 20

    Peanut Butter Ice Cream 22

    Chocolate Espresso Sorbet 23

    Coconut Ice Cream 25

    Macadamia White Chocolate Ice Cream 26

    Minty Chip Ice Cream 28

    Chunky Walnut Ice cream 30

    Cheesecake Ice Cream 32

Strawberry Ice Cream 34

Roasted Almond Bars Ice Cream 38

Matcha Green Tea Ice Cream 40

Neapolitan Ice Cream 42

Basil Ice Cream 44

Chai Latte Ice Cream 46

Coffee Caramel Ice Cream 48

Avo Lemon Ice Cream 51

Nutella Ice Cream 53

Hazelnut Ice Cream 55

Cinnamon French Vanilla Ice Cream 57

Loaf Pan Ice Cream 59

Salted Caramel Ice Cream 61

Chocolate Bacon Ice Cream 63

Rocky Choco Ice Cream 65

Blueberry Ice Cream 67

Irish Cream Ice Cream 69

Blue Delight Ice Cream 71

Double Dark Chocolate Ice Cream 73

Dulce De Leche With Salted Walnut Ice Cream........................ 75

Mocha Almond Ice Cream 77

Orange Dark Chocolate Ice Cream 79

Cotton Candy Ice Cream 81

Cinnamon Apple Ice Cream... 83

White Chocolate Peppermint Ice Cream 85

Raspberry Ice Cream 88

White Chocolate Raspberry Ice Cream 90

Avocado Ice Cream 92

Gingerbread Ice Cream 94

Peach Ice Cream 96

Pina Colada Ice Cream.. 98

Black Sesame Ice Cream 100

Vanilla Cake Ice Cream... 103

Fried Vanilla Ice Cream 104

Brownie Ice Cream 106

Maple Bacon Ice Cream 108

Almond Milk Ice Cream.. 110

Fatty Coconut Cream Ice Cream 113

Cookies and Cream Ice Cream..115

Saffron and Rosewater Persian Ice Cream........................... 118

Cereal Ice Cream...120

Peanut Butter and Jelly Ice Cream... 122

S'mores Ice Cream 124

Strawberry Rhubarb Ice Cream.. 126

Chocolate Banana Walnut Ice Cream..................................... 129

Cream Cannoli Ice Cream...131

Snicker Ice Cream 132

Cranberry and Rum Ice Cream.. 134

Orange and Dark Chocolate Ice Cream 136

Cherry Kefir Ice Cream 138

Red Velvet Ice Cream Cake... 139

Brown Butter Bourbon Pecan Ice Cream 143

Orange and Black Licorice Ice Cream 145

Maple Habanero Ice Cream...148

Green Chili and Mint Ice Cream 149

Cauliflower Ice Cream 151

Garlic Ice Cream 153

Wasabi and Cucumber Ice Cream 155

Black Charcoal Ice Cream 157

Dark Cherry and Chocolate Chunk Ice Cream 159

Amarenata Cherry Ice Cream 161

Lavender Wild Berry Ice Cream 164

Cheddar Cheese Ice Cream 166

Guava and Cream Cheese Ice Cream 168

Conclusion 170

Disclaimer

Copyright © 2020

All Rights Reserved.

No part of this book can be transmitted or reproduced in any form including print, electronic, photocopying, scanning, mechanical or recording without prior written permission from the author.

While the author has taken utmost efforts to ensure the accuracy of the written content, all readers are advised to follow information mentioned herein at their own risk. The author cannot be held responsible for any personal or commercial damage caused by information. All readers are encouraged to seek professional advice when needed.

Introduction

Ice cream! Ice cream! We all scream for ice cream!

If you ever thought you could never eat ice cream again- unless it came with a massive portion of guilt and weight gain, be prepared to be surprised!

Who doesn't like ice creams? Ice cream is the perfect comfort food, a refreshing snack on a hot day, and an extremely beloved sweet treat. Unfortunately, most of the ice creams available on the market these days are loaded with unhealthy sugars and preservatives. Also, have you ever encountered a diet that lets you eat ice creams? Probably not. Well, be prepared to be surprised!

What if I told you ice creams could be healthy? What if ice creams can be a part of your weight loss regime? What if ice creams can be made at home within no time? Do you want to eat ice creams without feeling guilty? What if ice creams could help attain your overall fitness and weight loss objectives? Are you wondering how this is possible? The answer to these questions is to turn toward keto ice creams. As the name suggests, the ice creams are designed in accordance with the ketogenic diet protocols. So, you can eat ice creams without compromising on your diet or taste buds! Are you wondering where you can look for all these recipes? Look no further, because this is the perfect book for you!

The keto or ketogenic diet is a high-fat and low-carb diet. It is one of the most popular diets these days, and it is here to stay. Unlike fad diets, which make tall claims but fail to deliver, the keto diet is truly brilliant. The keto diet is believed to assist with fat loss, weight loss maintenance, stabilizing blood sugar and cholesterol levels, improving cardiovascular health, better digestion, and strengthening the immune system. There are no hard and fast rules about calorie consumption. All you need to do is merely consume foods rich in healthy dietary fats while drastically reducing your carbs intake.

On a typical keto diet, about 70-75% of your daily calorie intake is obtained from dietary fats, 20% from protein, and the rest from carbs. This diet also prohibits or limits the consumption of unhealthy junk food. Most of the ready-to-eat food products flooding the market these days are rich in calories and barely contain any nutrients. Poor lifestyle choices, especially the diet we consume these days, are the leading reason for various problems plaguing humanity. The good news is you have the power to change things for the better.

The recipes given in this book are extremely simple to understand and easy to follow. Making ice creams has never been this fun or easy before. What more? The ice creams are 100% healthy and keto-friendly. They are made using healthy ingredients and don't have any preservatives. By making ice creams at home, you finally have complete control over the ingredients used. Carefully go through the different recipes given in this book, gather the required ingredients, pick a recipe, and follow the ingredients. You will be digging into a bowl of delicious, sweet, creamy, and cold goodness without any guilt within no time!

A brilliant thing about the keto recipes given in this book is they are made using low-carb or no-carb ingredients. It doesn't take any specific level of skill or expertise to make these ice creams. It requires minimal prep, and you don't have to wait for hours together to eat fresh and delicious homemade ice creams. The collection of recipes given in this book certainly makes things easy. You no longer have to search for any specific recipes online! From chocolaty to minty and fruity flavors, there is a lot to explore. You will certainly find a recipe that will tickle your fancy and taste buds.

Are you eager to jump into the world of delicious goodness? If you want to attain your weight loss, fitness, or health goals while eating healthy and delicious ice creams, it is time to get started immediately!

Keto Ice Cream Recipes

Pumpkin Spiced Pecan Pie Ice Cream

Serves: 04

Ingredients:

- 1/2 cup pumpkin puree
- 1-1/2 cups coconut milk, unsweetened
- 3 egg yolks
- 1/2 cup cottage cheese
- 1/2 cup pecans
- 1/2 cup xanthan gum
- 2 tbsp. salted butter
- 1/3 cup erythritol
- 8 drops liquid stevia
- 1 tsp. pumpkin spice
- 1 tsp. maple extract

Directions:

1. Toast pecans in a dry skillet for 3 minutes and then chop them.
2. In a saucepan, add butter and chopped pecans. Keep stirring for 2-3 minutes.
3. Add the rest of the ingredients into a large bowl and blend together using a hand blender.
4. Pour mixture into ice cream machine and let it churn for about 30 minutes or until it reaches consistency of soft ice. Add butter and pecans and churn for another 2 minutes.
5. Pour into a container and place it in the freezer for 2 hours.

Chocolate Therapy

Serves: 05

Ingredients:

- 1-1/4 cups of heavy cream
- 1/4 cup erythritol
- 2 egg yolks
- 1.5 tbsp. cocoa powder, unsweetened
- 1/2 tsp. vanilla extract

Directions:

1. In a saucepan, heat heavy cream and vanilla on low heat until it starts to simmer. Remove it from heat and let it cool until it is lukewarm.
2. Whisk egg yolks and erythritol together until it changes color to pale yellow. Add cocoa powder and give it a good mix until it is lump free.

3. Add half of the cream mixture into eggs and mix well. Ensure cream is not too hot or it will begin to cook the eggs and form lumps. Whisk continuously.
4. Return the mixture to the saucepan and let it thicken on low heat. Stir continuously. This process may take 15-20 minutes and you would know the doneness once the mixture starts to coat back of a spoon instead of dripping.
5. Pour mixture into a container and freeze until it is completely cooled. Stir every 10 minutes to fasten the process.
6. In an ice cream churner, pour mixture once it is cold and let it churn for 30 minutes.
7. Once it comes to a soft consistency, pour it back in the container and freeze it for 15 minutes or until it is hard.

Snow White Vanilla

Serves: 04

Ingredients:

Ice cream
- 2 egg yolks
- 1/4 cup sugar free vanilla syrup
- 3/4 cup heavy cream
- 1/2 tsp. vanilla extract
- 1 tsp. Vodka, optional

Sugar free vanilla syrup

- 3/4 cup xylitol
- 2 tsp. vanilla essence
- 1/8 tsp. xanthan gum
- 1 cup water

Directions:

1. In a saucepan, mix xylitol, xanthan gum, vanilla essence and whisk to make sugar free vanilla syrup. Add 1 cup water.
2. Bring it to a boil and let it simmer for 2-3 minutes. We will be using 1/4 cup for this recipe, set aside until it becomes lukewarm. Rest syrup once completely cooled can be stored in an airtight container and used in other recipes.
3. In a mixing bowl, add egg yolks and whisk with a hand mixer on medium speed. Slowly pour 1/4 cup warm vanilla syrup. Add vodka and beat it until it is thick and creamy.
4. In another bowl, whisk cream until it forms stiff peaks. Fold cream mixture into egg mixture and combine well.
5. Transfer to a metal container, freeze for 4-6 hours and enjoy.

Lemon Ice Cream

Serves: 04

Ingredients:

- 2/3 tbsp. lemon juice and zest
- 1-1/4 cup heavy whipping cream
- 2 whole eggs
- 3/4 cup heavy cream
- 1/4 cup erythritol
- Yellow food color, optional

Directions:

1. Separate eggs in 2 mixing bowls. With a hand mixer, beat egg whites until they form a stiff peak. In another bowl, whisk egg yolk and erythritol until it becomes fluffy. Add lemon juice and yellow food color to egg yolk mixture.
2. Fold egg whites into egg yolk mixture and add lemon zest to it.

3. Whip cream in a large bowl until it becomes soft and light. Now fold egg mixture into this.
4. Place bowl in the freezer and stir every 20-30 minutes until it gets to ice cream consistency. It could take anywhere between 2-3 hours.
5. Place it at room temperature 15 minutes before serving.

Sky Cheese Ice Cream

Serves: 04

Ingredients:

- 1/2 cup frozen blueberries
- 2/3 cup heavy whipping cream
- 1/2 cup mascarpone cheese
- 2 egg yolks
- 1/3 tsp. ground green cardamom
- 1/3 zest of lemon
- 3/4 cup heavy cream
- 1/2 tsp vanilla extract
- 2/3 tbsp. erythritol, optional

Directions:

1. Take frozen blueberries out from the freezer and keep it aside until it is half-thawed.
2. Whisk heavy cream until it turns fluffy.

3. In a mixing bowl add egg yolks, erythritol, vanilla extract, cardamom and lemon zest, beat it with hand mixer until fluffy and pale yellow in color. Add mascarpone cheese and mix until incorporated.
4. In the same mixture, fold whipped cream and then half-thawed blueberries.
5. Pour mixture in a container and freeze. Stir every 15-20 minutes until it firms up.
6. Continue freezing for 2 more hours.

Peanut Butter Ice Cream

Serves: 04

Ingredients:

- 1-1/2 cup full fat coconut milk, chilled
- 3/4 cup peanut butter
- 1/2 cup mascarpone cheese
- 1/4 cup keto maple syrup

Directions:

1. Keep a container/loaf pan in the freezer for 3-4 hours or overnight.
2. Add all ingredients and blend it until thick and creamy.
3. Pour ice cream mixture in the chilled container.
4. Stir ice cream every 15-20 minutes for about 2 hours. Let it further freeze for 3 hours.

Chocolate Espresso Sorbet

Serves: 06

Ingredients:

- 1 cup strong brewed coffee
- 1-1/2 bars of 90% dark chocolate, finely chopped
- 6 tbsp. erythritol
- ½ tbsp. vegetable glycerin
- 5 drops liquid stevia
- 1 tbsp. cocoa powder
- 2 cups water

Directions:

1. In a saucepan add coffee, vegetable glycerin, sweeteners and water. Heat until dissolved.
2. In a heatproof bowl, place finely chopped chocolate bars & cocoa powder.
3. Pour hot coffee mixture over chocolate and stir until melted.

4. Once combined, pour mixture into a metal container and freeze it overnight or for 8 hours.
5. Cut frozen mixture in small squares by a knife and blend in a food processor until it is smooth and creamy. Pour it back into a metal container. This step will ensure a smooth texture of Ice cream.
6. Freeze until firm enough to be scooped.

Coconut Ice Cream

Serves: 05

Ingredients:

- 7 tbsp. cashew butter or almond butter
- 1 cup coconut full fat milk, chilled
- 2 tbsp. keto maple syrup
- 2 tbsp. coconut flakes
- 1/2 tsp. coconut extract

Directions:

1. Keep a container/loaf pan in the freezer for 4-6 hours before starting the process.
2. In a blender, mix butter, coconut milk, maple syrup and coconut extract. Blend until smooth and creamy.
3. Pour ice cream mixture in a chilled container.
4. Stir ice cream every 15-20 minutes for an initial 2 hours.
5. Continue freezing for 3 hours more.
6. Garnish with coconut flakes before serving.

Macadamia White Chocolate Ice Cream

Serves: 04

Ingredients:

- 1 cup coconut milk
- 1 egg
- 2 egg yolks
- 1/2 cup macadamia nuts, toasted and salted
- 1/4 cup cacao butter, sugar-free
- 3 tbsp. erythritol
- 10 drops stevia
- 1 tsp. vanilla extract
- 1/4 tsp. xanthan gum

Directions:

1. In a food processor make a paste of macadamia nuts.
2. Melt cacao butter in a saucepan on low heat.
3. In a large bowl add egg yolks, stevia and vanilla extract. Blend until it turns pale yellow and smooth.

4. In another bowl, whisk egg whites until fluffy. Add coconut milk and whisk until it thickens.
5. Fold egg yolks mixture into coconut milk mixture until completely incorporated.
6. Pour in a container and freeze for 1 hour.
7. Add the same to the ice cream machine and churn as per instructions.
8. Eat immediately if you prefer soft ice cream or freeze for 1 hour.

Minty Chip Ice Cream

Serves: 04

Ingredients:

- 1 cup heavy whipping cream
- 1 tbsp. butter
- 2 tbsp. chocolate chips
- 1/4 tsp. peppermint extract
- 3 tbsp. powdered erythritol
- 2 drops green food color, optional

Directions:

1. In a saucepan, melt chocolate chips and butter and stir it occasionally.
2. Add 1 tbsp. whipping cream to it.
3. Spread mixture into metal container/loaf over parchment paper and freeze it for 30 minutes or until solid.
4. Combine the remaining heavy cream, peppermint extract, erythritol and green food color in a large bowl. Blend until

it doubles in size and gets to consistency of soft ice. It may take 3-5 minutes.
5. Remove chocolate from the freezer, slice into small squares with a knife. Fold into a heavy cream mixture.
6. Allow to freeze for 5 hours before serving.

Chunky Walnut Ice cream

Serves: 04

Ingredients:

- 1/2 almond milk, unsweetened
- 6 tbsp. erythritol
- 1 large egg
- 1 cup heavy whipping cream
- 1-1/2 tsp. unflavored gelatin
- 1/4 cup chopped walnuts
- 1/4 tsp. banana extract/flavoring
- 3 tbsp. stevia sweetened dark chocolate
- 1/2 tsp. vanilla extract

Directions:

1. Whisk erythritol and gelatin in a large saucepan.
2. Add almond milk & egg to mixture and whisk. Keep stirring continuously on low heat.

3. Remove from heat when it starts to simmer. Place it in ice cold water.
4. When mixture gets to room temperature, whisk whipped cream, banana extract and vanilla extract.
5. Pour mixture into the ice cream machine and follow instructions.
6. When it reaches desired consistency, add chopped walnuts and chocolate pieces and let it churn for another 2 minutes.
7. Transfer mixture to metal container. Cover and place it in the freezer.
8. Let it sit for 2-3 hours before serving.

Cheesecake Ice Cream

Serves: 05

Ingredients:

- 1-1/4 cup heavy cream
- 1/4 cup, keto-friendly shortbread cookies
- 1/2 cup cream cheese
- 2 egg yolks
- 1 cup light whipping cream
- 1/2 cup Natvia sweetener
- 1/2 tsp. vanilla extract
- 1 tbsp. lemon juice

Directions:

1. In a saucepan, heat whipping cream until it starts to steam.
2. Combine egg yolks, cream cheese, Natvia and vanilla extract in a bowl. Blend with a hand mixer until all ingredients come together.

3. Pour 1/4 of warm cream into egg mixture and mix well. Pour remaining cream and combine. Transfer it to a saucepan.
4. On low heat, stir the mixture continuously to avoid scrambling. It is done when it turns into custard consistency.
5. Pour custard in a heat proof bowl and stir for 5 minutes before placing in the fridge. Let it chill for 10-15 minutes.
6. Whip heavy cream until it reaches soft peaks.
7. Remove custard from the fridge, add lemon juice and mix.
8. Fold in whipped cream to custard in 2 batches.
9. Pour mixture into the ice cream machine and let it churn for 30 minutes.
10. Freeze mixture for 1 hour
11. Top it up by keto shortbread cookies for the crunch and serve.

Strawberry Ice Cream

Serves: 05

Ingredients:

- 3/4 cups full fat sour cream
- 1.5 cups fresh strawberries
- 3/4 cup Heavy cream
- 2 tbsp. xylitol
- 3-1/4 tbsp. powdered erythritol
- 1/2 tsp. vanilla essence
- 2 tbsp. vodka, optional

Directions:

1. Blend strawberries and xylitol in a food processor until almost pureed but with some chunks remaining.
2. Whisk together strawberry mixture, sour cream, vanilla extract and vodka until combined.
3. In another large bowl, whisk heavy cream with erythritol until it forms stiff peaks.

4. Fold whipped cream into strawberry mixture.
5. Transfer mixture to a bowl; place it in the freezer for 5-6 hours and serve.

Chunky walnut Maple Ice cream

Serves: 04

Ingredients:

- 1-1/4 cups full heavy whipping cream
- 1/4 cup chopped walnuts
- 2 tbsp. keto friendly brown sugar
- 2 tbsp. xylitol
- 1 tbsp. butter
- 1 tsp. maple extract
- 2 tbsp. xanthan gum

Directions:

1. In a medium saucepan on medium heat, add half of whipping cream, xylitol and brown sugar. Simmer for 30 minutes, not boil. Small bubbles should be seen on the edges throughout.
2. Whisk butter and maple extract in whipping cream mixture once removed from heat.

3. Sprinkle xanthan gum in batches, whisk continuously.
4. Once it comes to room temperature, refrigerate mixture for 2 hours.
5. Beat the remaining half of whipping cream with a hand blender until it forms stiff peaks.
6. Fold in chilled maple mixture & chopped walnuts into whipping cream mixture.
7. Place it in the freezer in an airtight container for 5 hours and serve.

Roasted Almond Bars Ice Cream

Serves: 05 bars

Ingredients:

- 3/4 cup heavy cream
- 3/4 cup ground almonds
- 1 tsp. pure almond extract
- 1 tsp. fresh lime juice
- 2 tbsp. keto friendly brown sugar

Directions:

1. In a dry skillet roast ground almond for approximately 5 minutes over medium to low heat, stir continuously so it doesn't burn.
2. Whip heavy cream and sugar in a large bowl until it is light and soft.
3. Add fresh lime juice and almond extract to the mixture and stir.

4. In the ice cream mold, add 1 spoon roasted almond and then top it with whipped cream mixture and repeat the process one more time for the same mold and likewise for all.
5. Freeze the ice cream molds until firm for 5-6 hours.
6. Remove ice cream bars from mold and enjoy.

Matcha Green Tea Ice Cream

Serves: 04

Ingredients:

- 1/4 cup almond butter or cashew or pistachio butter
- 1-1/2 cup full fat coconut milk
- 1 tbsp. matcha powder
- 1/4 cup erythritol
- 1 tbsp. vodka
- 1/4 tsp. xanthan gum
- 1/4 tsp. powdered xylitol

Directions:

1. Mix all ingredients in a large bowl and blend it with a hand blender or in a food processor for 1 minute.
2. Pour batter into an airtight container and refrigerate for 2 hours.

3. After 2 hours whisk again it in a large bowl and freeze it covered for approximately 6 hours. Give it a mix every hour until it gets very firm to avoid forming ice crystals.
4. Take out from the freezer and keep it at room temperature for 10 minutes before serving.

Neapolitan Ice Cream

Serves: 04

Ingredients:

- 1/2 cup + 2 tbsp. heavy whipping cream
- 2 eggs, separated
- 1 cup strawberries
- 3 tbsp. powdered erythritol
- 1/8 cup cacao powder
- 1/8 tsp. apple cider vinegar
- 1/2 tbsp. vanilla extract

Directions:

1. **Vanilla base.** Whisk egg whites with apple cider vinegar. Once thickens, add erythritol. Whisk until it forms stiff peaks.
2. In a large bowl whisk whipped cream until soft peaks are formed.
3. Mix egg yolks and vanilla extract in a small bowl.

4. Fold whisked eggs mixture into whipped cream. Add egg yolk and combine.
5. Divide vanilla base mixture in 3 parts.
6. **Strawberry base**. Blend smooth fresh strawberries in a food processed after removing green ends.
7. Pour blended strawberries in one part of the vanilla base and gently fold with spatula.
8. **Chocolate base**. Sift cacao powder in the third part of the vanilla base and fold gently.
9. **Assemble**: In a freezer friendly metal pan/loaf add chocolate layer and spread evenly. Now add strawberry base and finally vanilla base. Maintain the same order as it is done considering the consistency of each base.
10. Freeze for 4 hours, once set cut in slices and serve.

Basil Ice Cream

Serves: 04

Ingredients:

- 1/2 cup fresh basil
- 1 can full fat coconut milk, unsweetened
- 1 egg yolk
- 1/2 tbsp. lemon zest
- 1/4 cup erythritol

Directions:

1. Blend 1/4 cup coconut milk and basil in the food processor until smooth.
2. Prepare a double boiler on low heat, place basil milk, remaining coconut milk, lemon zest and erythritol. Let it simmer for 5-7 minutes. Do not let it boil.
3. In a separate bowl, beat egg yolk.
4. Add 1/4 basil mixture to beaten yolk and whisk continuously. Pour it back in the double boiler and let it

cook until it reaches thick consistency. Stir frequently to avoid the egg from scrambling or forming lumps.
5. Strain through a fine sieve and refrigerate mixture for 2 hours.
6. Transfer mixture into Ice cream maker and churn for 30 minutes.
7. Freeze in an airtight container for 2 hours.
8. Before serving, set it out at room temperature for 10 minutes.

Chai Latte Ice Cream

Serves: 04

Ingredients:

- 2 black tea bags
- 1/8 cup monkfruit sweetener
- 1 cup full fat coconut milk
- 1 tsp. vanilla extract
- 1/2 tsp. ground nutmeg
- 1/4 tsp. black pepper
- 1/4 tsp. ground cardamom
- 1/2 tsp. ground ginger
- 1-1/2 tsp. ground cinnamon
- 1/4 tsp. ground cloves
- 2 drops stevia
- Pinch of salt

Directions:

1. Into a saucepan on low heat, add 1/2 cup coconut milk and monk fruit sweetener. Take off heat when it starts steaming.
2. Steep tea bags for 10-15 minutes in coconut milk mixture, squeeze tea bags when removing to get all the juice.
3. Blend tea mixture, remaining coconut milk, all spices and other ingredients in a blender until smooth.
4. Pour mixture into your Ice cream machine and churn as per instructions.
5. Freeze the mixture for 4-5 hours. Let it sit at room temperature for 10 minutes before serving.

Coffee Caramel Ice Cream

Serves: 06

Ingredients:

Coffee paste
- 1/2 tbsp. instant coffee
- 1/2 tbsp. water

Caramel sauce
- 3 tbsp. heavy cream
- 1/2 tsp. instant coffee
- 2 tbsp. erythritol
- 2 tbsp. xylitol
- 1 tbsp. butter
- 2 tbsp. stevia
- Pinch of salt

Ice cream base
- 1 cup heavy cream
- 2 egg yolks
- 3/4 cup Almond milk, unsweetened
- 1/2 tbsp. vegetable glycerin

- 2 tbsp. erythritol
- 2 tsp. xylitol

Directions:

1. **Caramel**: Into a saucepan combine 2 tbsp. heavy cream, 1 tbsp butter and sweeteners, combine over low heat stirring continuously. It is done when it starts to bubble, changes its color to lightly brown and thick.
2. Remove from heat. Add remaining heavy cream, butter, instant coffee and salt.
3. Stir until it becomes smooth and let cool.
4. **Ice cream**: In a blender, add heavy cream, almond milk, sweeteners, egg yolks and glycerin. Blend until smooth and transfer to Ice cream maker. Churn as per instructions of the Ice cream manufacturer.
5. **Coffee paste**: mix instant coffee and water until a thick paste is formed. Add more water if required.
6. Once the ice cream is almost done, take half of it to place it in the pan and freeze. Add coffee paste to balance ice cream and churn for another 10 minutes.

7. Remove pan from freezer, pour balance ice cream on top and give it a swirl. With a butter knife, make zig zag lines and pour caramel mixture.
8. Give it a very gentle swirl.
9. Freeze for 4 hours and serve.

Avo Lemon Ice Cream

Serves: 04

Ingredients:

- 3 avocados, medium
- 1-1/2 tbsp. MCT oil
- 1/4 tsp. stevia
- 1 cup water
- 3/4 lemon juice
- 2 tsp. gelatin
- 2 tbsp. ground cashew / almond

Directions:

1. Blend avocado, water, lemon juice, stevia, ground cashew and MCT oil in a food processor until smooth.
2. Add gelatin while it is still blending.
3. Pour mixture into an Ice cream machine and churn as per instructions of the manufacturer or until it starts to get the consistency of soft serve.

4. Freeze it in an airtight container for 1 hours and serve.

Nutella Ice Cream

Serves: 05

Ingredients:

- 2 egg yolks
- 3/4 cup heavy whipping cream
- 6 tbsp. almond milk
- 3 tbsp. xylitol
- 2 tbsp. erythritol
- 3 tbsp. chopped keto brownies
- 2 tbsp. sugar free Nutella
- 1 tbsp. vodka, optional

Directions:

1. Place a bowl in the freezer to chill.

2. In a saucepan, combine and stir whipping cream, almond milk and sweeteners on medium heat.
3. Whisk egg yolks in a separate bowl, pour 1/4 cup whipping cream mixture into egg yolks. Whisk continuously. Return egg yolk mixture to the saucepan with the rest of the whipping cream and mix. Cook until mixture becomes thick and sticks to the back of a spoon/spatula.
4. Remove from heat, add Nutella and whisk.
5. Pour mixture in the chilled bowl and let it sit for 10 minutes.
6. Cover with cling wrap and refrigerate for 3-4 hours.
7. Transfer mixture to Ice cream maker, add vodka and churn as per manufacturer's instructions.
8. Freeze in an airtight container for 2 hours and serve.

Hazelnut Ice Cream

Serves: 04

Ingredients:

- 3/4 cup heavy whipping cream
- 1/2 cup ground hazelnut
- 6 tbsp. erythritol
- 1 tsp. vanilla extract
- 1 whole egg
- 1 egg yolk
- 1/4 cup chopped toasted hazelnut

Directions:

1. Into a small saucepan, roast ground hazelnut until they change color to golden yellow. Stir frequently to avoid burning.
2. Add heavy cream, roasted hazelnut and vanilla extract to a large pot on medium heat and bring it to boil. Keep stirring

3. Whisk egg yolks in a separate bowl with erythritol until they turn pale yellow.
4. Prepare a double boiler and place egg mixture on it. Once it comes to a boil, start adding hazelnut mixture slowly and mix.
5. Stir for 5-7 minutes until it starts to thicken and starts to coat the spatula.
6. Let the mixture cool down, then add chopped hazelnuts. Combine and refrigerate for 30-45 minutes.
7. Add vodka, mix and freeze in an airtight container for 5-6 hours. Stir every 30 minutes for an initial 2 hours.

Cinnamon French Vanilla Ice Cream

Serves: 04

Ingredients:

- 1-1/2 cup heavy whipping cream
- 6 tbsp. unsweetened almond milk
- 1/4 cup erythritol
- 1/4 cup xylitol
- 3 drops MCT oil, vanilla flavored
- 8 drops hazelnut flavor
- 1/ 2 scoop French vanilla protein powder

Directions:

1. Whisk whipping cream in a large mixing bowl until it forms stiff peaks.
2. Add erythritol, xylitol and MCT vanilla oil to the heavy cream mixture and beat until mixed.

3. In a small bowl, mix protein powder and almond milk, add hazelnut drops and combine.
4. When the mixture turns smooth, pour it into Ice cream maker and churn until it becomes solid consistency.
5. Transfer mixture to freezer in an airtight container and allow it to set for 6-7 hours.
6. Place it at room temperature for 10 minutes before serving.

Loaf Pan Ice Cream

Serves: 04

Ingredients:

- 3/4 cup full fat coconut milk
- 6 tbsp. erythritol
- 1/4 cup keto friendly dark chocolate nibs
- Pinch of salt
- 1 cup heavy whipping cream
- 2 tbsp. xanthan gum
- 3 tsp. vanilla essence

Directions:

1. Place a loaf pan in the freezer to chill.
2. In a saucepan over medium heat add coconut milk, sweetener and salt. Whisk until all solids are dissolved and the mixture is smooth.

3. Sprinkle xanthan gum little by little until combined.
4. Sieve mixture in a bowl and cover by cling wrap directly on the mixture. Allow it to cool completely. It will have jelly like texture.
5. Whip heavy cream in a bowl until it forms soft peaks.
6. Mix in keto friendly dark chocolate nibs, vanilla mixture and vanilla extract to heavy cream. Add chilled coconut milk mixture and blend until it is well incorporated.
7. Transfer mixture into chilled loaf pan, cover and freeze for 4 hours.

Salted Caramel Ice Cream

Serves: 04

Ingredients:

Ice cream
- 1-1/2 tsp sugar free caramel syrup
- 1 egg yolk
- 1 whole egg
- 1/2 cup heavy cream
- 1 tbsp. golden monk fruit sweetener
- 1 tsp. vanilla extract
- 1-1/2 tbsp. erythritol
- Pinch of flakey sea salt

Caramel chunks
- 1-1/2 tbsp. nut butter-almond/cashew/peanut butter
- 1-1/2 tbsp. golden monk fruit sweetener
- 1-1/2 tbsp. melted butter
- 1-1/2 tsp. sugar free caramel syrup

Directions:

1. Add heavy cream, vanilla extract and salt to a large pot on medium heat and bring it to boil. Keep stirring
2. Whisk egg yolks in a separate bowl with erythritol until they turn pale yellow.
3. Prepare a double boiler and in a large pot place egg mixture on top. Once it comes to a boil, start adding heavy cream mixture slowly and combine.
4. Stir for 5-7 minutes until it thickens and starts to coat the spatula.
5. Let the mixture cool, add sugar free caramel syrup, combine and refrigerate for 30-45 minutes.
6. Add vodka, mix and freeze in an airtight container for 5-6 hours. Stir every 30 minutes for the first 2 hours.
7. After 4 hours, mix ingredients of caramel chunks and add it to the ice cream. Give it a good stir.
8. Keep the ice cream at room temperature for 10-15 mins before serving.

Chocolate Bacon Ice Cream

Serves: 04

Ingredients:

- 3/4 cup heavy whipping cream
- 1/2 cup almond milk, unsweetened
- 1/2 cup cocoa powder, sugar-free
- 2 tbsp. crispy bacon, chopped
- 2 whole eggs
- 1/2 cup Erythritol
- 1/4 tsp. xanthan gum
- 2 spoons sugar free toffee, chopped
- 2 pieces of 90% dark chocolate sugar free
- Pinch of salt

Directions:

1. In a blender/food processor combine erythritol, almond milk, xanthan gum, cocoa powder and eggs. Blend until smooth.

2. Transfer mixture to microwave safe bowl and microwave for 30 seconds and stir, repeat this process 3 times until the mixture thickens.
3. Whisk in heavy whipping cream and salt.
4. Place in the refrigerator for 3 hours.
5. In a saucepan, melt chocolate, with 2 tbsp. heavy cream and then stir in chopped bacon.
6. Pour mixture on parchment paper and freeze until it becomes hard. Chop and set aside once hardened.
7. Remove Ice cream mixture and transfer to Ice cream churner and churn until it comes to desired consistency. Once it is almost done, add chopped chocolate and bacon along with chopped toffee and churn for 2-3 minutes.
8. Freeze the mixture for 4 hours and serve.

Rocky Choco Ice Cream

Serves: 04

Ingredients:

- 1/4 cup chopped raw almonds
- 1/4 cup sugar free marshmallow, cut in small pieces
- 1 cup heavy whipping cream
- 2 tbsp. cocoa powder, sugar-free
- 2 tbsp. + 2 tsp. swerve sugar substitute
- 1 tsp. vanilla extract
- 1/4 tsp. xanthan gum
- Pinch of salt

Directions:

1. In a blender/food processor combine all ingredients apart from marshmallows and almonds. Beat on high speed until thick.
2. Transfer the mixture to an airtight container; fold in the marshmallows and almonds.

3. Cover and freeze ice cream for 4 hours and serve.

Blueberry Ice Cream

Serves: 04

Ingredients:

- 1-3/4 cup full fat coconut milk, chilled
- 3/4 cup cashews, soaked overnight
- 1-1/2 cup blueberries, frozen
- 2 tbsp. fresh lemon juice
- 1/4 cup liquid keto friendly sugar substitute
- 1 tsp. vanilla extract
- Pinch of salt

Directions:

1. Place the Ice cream container in the freezer a night before you want to make the ice cream. Also soak cashews and keep coconut milk to chill.
2. Blend all ingredients with a hand mixer/food processor except coconut milk.

3. Remove coconut cans from the fridge, extract hardened part of the coconut milk and place it in a bowl. We will not be using the liquid part for this recipe.
4. Whisk coconut milk until soft and fluffy.
5. Fold in blueberries; add small quantities at a time.
6. Transfer mixture to the container that is chilled overnight and let it freeze for 1 hour.
7. Remove and stir to break any ice formed.
8. Freeze for 4-5 hours, stir it every 30 mins until it gets a smooth texture like soft Ice or soft serve.
9. Keep it at room temperature 10 minutes before serving.

Irish Cream Ice Cream

Serves: 04

Ingredients:

- 1/2 cup Irish whiskey
- 1/2 cup full fat coconut milk, unsweetened
- 1 cup heavy whipping cream
- 1/2 tsp. instant espresso
- 1 tsp. cocoa powder, unsweetened
- 1 tsp. almond extract
- 1 tsp. vanilla extract
- 3 tbsp. erythritol
- 1/4 cup powdered monk fruit
- Pinch of salt

Directions:

1. **Irish cream**: In a blender, mix 1/2 cup heavy cream, Irish whiskey, monk fruit, cocoa powder, 1/2 tsp. vanilla

extract, 1 tsp. almond extract, instant espresso and mix until smooth.
2. In a large bowl, whisk the remaining heavy cream until it forms soft peaks and becomes fluffy.
3. Fold in 1/2 cup of Irish cream mixture into cream until combined.
4. Transfer in an airtight container and freeze the same for 3 – 4 hours.
5. Stir after every 30 mins for an initial 2 hours and serve.
6. Remaining Irish cream can be stored for up to 7 days and be used for cocktails/shakes.

Blue Delight Ice Cream

Serves: 04

Ingredients:

- 1 cup heavy cream
- 1/4 tsp. orange extract
- 1/4 tsp. raspberry extract
- 1/8 tsp. fresh lemon juice.
- 1/8 tsp. almond extract
- 2 egg yolks
- 1/3 cup monk fruit sweetener
- Blue food color, recommended but optional

Directions:

1. In a saucepan on medium heat, boil heavy cream and sweetener. Let it simmer until it thickens.
2. Remove from heat and let it cool completely.
3. Mix egg yolks, all extracts, lemon juice and blue color in a bowl.

4. Pour in half of the egg mixture in heavy cream when it is completely cooled. Combine well. Now add the rest of the egg mixture and whisk.
5. Transfer mixture into an airtight container/metal pan and freeze for 4 hours.
6. Stir the mixture every 30 minutes for the first 2 hours.

Double Dark Chocolate Ice Cream

Serves: 04

Ingredients:

- 3 tbsp. cocoa powder
- 1-1/4 cup heavy cream
- 1 tsp. vanilla extract
- 1/2 cup sugar free dark chocolate
- Pinch of salt
- 1/4 cup erythritol
- 1 tbsp. vodka or gin, optional

Directions:

1. Place the freezer safe metal container in the freezer a night before.
2. In a saucepan, melt dark chocolate on low heat and let it cool
3. Whisk heavy cream, erythritol and vanilla extract in the chilled container until it is soft and fluffy.

4. Add melted chocolate, cocoa powder, pinch of salt and vodka. Mix well.
5. Pour mixture into a metal pan/airtight container and freeze for 5-6 hours.
6. Stir the mixture every 30 minutes for first 2 hours.

Dulce De Leche With Salted Walnut Ice Cream

Serves: 05

Ingredients:

- 1 cup low fat dulce de leche
- 1 cup heavy cream
- 1/8 tsp. stevia extract
- 1/8 tsp. xanthan gum
- 1 tsp. vanilla extract
- 6 tbsp. roughly chopped walnut
- 1/2 tbsp. melted butter
- 2 tbsp. vodka, optional
- Pinch of salt

Directions:

1. Mix chopped walnuts, butter and salt on a baking tray and place it in a preheated oven.
2. Toss after every minute until golden brown, this could take 10-15 minutes. Remove from the oven and let it cool.

3. Whisk dulce de leche, vanilla extract, stevia and heavy cream in a large bowl until combined. Add vodka to mixture.
4. Sprinkle xanthan gum in batches and whisk to combine.
5. Add roasted walnuts and stir.
6. Freeze for 4-5 hours; stir the mixture every 30 minutes for initial 2 hours.
7. Remove and keep at room temperature for 10 minutes before serving.

Mocha Almond Ice Cream

Serves: 04

Ingredients:

- 3 tbsp. chopped almonds
- 1-1/2 tbsp. cocoa powder
- 1 cup heavy cream
- 1/2 cup sugar free mocha latte shake
- 1 large egg yolk
- 1 whole egg
- 1/8 cup powdered erythritol
- Pinch of salt

Directions:

1. Whisk together mocha shake and heavy cream in a saucepan on medium heat. Stir continuously; you should see small bubbles on the edge while steaming. Do not let it boil. This could take 5-7 minutes.

2. Whisk eggs together, add powdered erythritol and cocoa powder. Whisk again until well combined.
3. Once mocha mixture is cooled, pour 1/2 cup over whisked eggs and mix. Now pour this egg mixture along with the remaining mocha mixture in the saucepan.
4. Stir continuously until thick and it starts to coat the back of the spatula. It will turn into custard like consistency.
5. Transfer mixture in a bowl, cling wrap directly on the mixture and not the bowl to avoid the surface of mixture from hardening. Refrigerate for 4-5 hours.
6. Pour into a metal pan/airtight container and freeze mixture for 5-6 hours. For the first 2 hours, stir every 30 minutes to avoid forming of ice. Add chopped almonds after 1-1/2 hour, stir it again and continue freezing.
7. Remove and place at room temperature 10 minutes before serving.

Orange Dark Chocolate Ice Cream

Serves: 04

Ingredients:

- 2 tsp. orange zest
- 1-1/2 tbsp. cocoa powder
- 3/4 cup heavy cream
- 1/2 cup sugar free dark chocolate shake
- 1 egg yolk
- 1 whole egg
- 1/8 cup powdered erythritol
- 1/2 tsp. orange extract
- Pinch of salt

Directions:

1. Whisk together dark chocolate shake, orange zest and heavy cream in a saucepan on medium heat. Stir continuously; you should see small bubbles on the edge

and steaming. Do not let it boil. This could take 5-7 minutes.
2. Whisk eggs together, add powdered erythritol, orange extract and cocoa powder. Whisk again until well combined.
3. Once chocolate mixture is cooled, pour 1/2 cup over whisked eggs and mix. Now pour this egg mixture along with the remaining chocolate mixture in the saucepan.
4. Stir continuously until thick and it starts to coat the back of the spatula. It will turn into custard like consistency.
5. Transfer mixture in a bowl in an airtight container, refrigerated for 4 – 5 hours.
6. Stir the mixture and freeze for 5 - 6 hours. For the first 2 hours, stir every 30 minutes to avoid ice from forming. Add chopped almonds after 1-1/2 hour and then continue freezing.

Cotton Candy Ice Cream

Serves: 02

Ingredients:

- 1/2 cup heavy whipped cream
- 2 eggs, separated
- 1 tsp. MCT oil
- 1/8 tsp. xanthan gum
- 1/4 tsp. vanilla extract
- 1 drop each Pink and blue food color
- 1/2 tsp. erythritol
- 1/8 tsp. apple cider vinegar
- 1/2 tsp. cotton candy extract
- Pinch of salt

Directions:

1. **Base:** Whisk egg whites with apple cider vinegar. Once thickens, add erythritol. Whisk until it forms stiff peaks.

2. In a large bowl whisk whipped cream until soft peaks are formed.
3. Mix egg yolks and vanilla extract, cotton candy extract and MCT oil in a small bowl.
4. Fold whisked eggs mixture into whipped cream. Add egg yolk and combine. Sprinkle xanthan gum and whisk.
5. Divide base mixture in 3 parts.
6. Add pink and blue food color in 2 separate mixtures and mix until combined
7. In a freezer friendly metal pan/ loaf add base vanilla layer and spread evenly. Now make zigzag lines from the center and add pink base and repeat the same for blue base. Swirl it with butter knife so all colors are mixed well.
8. Freeze for 4 hours. If it gets too hard then keep 10 minutes at room temperature before serving.

Cinnamon Apple Ice Cream

Serves: 04

Ingredients:

- 3/4 cup heavy whipped cream
- 1 medium apple
- 1 egg yolk
- 1 whole egg
- 1/2 tsp. cinnamon powder
- 1 tbsp. erythritol
- 1/2 tsp. vanilla extract
- 2 tbsp. chopped apples, optional
- Pinch of salt

Directions:

1. Grate the apple. In a non-stick saucepan add heavy cream, grated apple, cinnamon and vanilla extract. Heat on medium flame until it comes to a boil.
2. Keep stirring while it begins to boil.

3. In a large bowl whisk eggs and erythritol until the color changes to pale yellow and it gets fluffy. Prepare a double boiler at home. Place the bowl with egg mixture on top and let the water get to a boil.
4. Add apple-cinnamon mixture to egg mixture in small batches and keep whisking. Stir for 5 minutes until it becomes thick and starts to stick to the back of the spatula.
5. Get if off the double boiler and let it cool down. Refrigerate it for 30 minutes.
6. Add vodka and give it a mix. Place the bowl in the freezer and keep stirring after every 30 minutes for the next 2 hours.
7. Let it freeze for a total of 5-6 hours for best results.
8. Keep it at room temperature for 10 minutes. Top it with chopped apple if you like and serve.

White Chocolate Peppermint Ice Cream

Serves: 04

Ingredients:

- 2 egg yolk
- 3 tbsp. powdered erythritol
- 4 drops unflavored liquid stevia
- 1/4 tsp. vanilla extract
- 3/4 tsp. peppermint extract
- 1/8 tsp. xanthan gum
- Pinch of red food color, optional
- 1/4 cup Cacao butter, squares
- 1-1/4 cup heavy whipped cream
- Pinch of salt

Directions:

1. In a non-stick saucepan heat half heavy cream until it simmers.

2. Whisk balance heavy cream in a bowl until soft peaks are formed.
3. Add egg yolks, erythritol, stevia, and xanthan gum, vanilla and salt in a bowl and whisk it. Slowly add the warm heavy cream mixture into the egg yolk mixture and whisk continuously to avoid scrambling of eggs.
4. To this mixture, add the remaining whipped cream and peppermint extract. Taste and adjust peppermint flavor as per liking.
5. Let the mixture sit in the fridge and chill for at least 3-4 hours.
6. Pour the same in an Ice cream maker and let it start churning.
7. Meanwhile prepare a double boiler and add cacao butter and erythritol and whisk until it melts and is smooth. Add food color and stir.
8. Let it cool slightly and pour the cacao butter mixture into the ice cream machine while it is churning. This will give a chunky white chocolate texture.
9. Churn total for 20 minutes and stop when it reaches consistency that is slightly thicker than soft serve.

10. Serve it immediately or transfer it to an airtight container and freeze it for 3-4 hours to reach the consistency of Ice cream.

Raspberry Ice Cream

Serves: 04

Ingredients:

- 3/4 cup heavy whipped cream
- 1 egg yolk
- 1 whole egg
- 1/4 cup raspberries
- 3 tbsp. erythritol
- 1/2 tsp. fresh lemon juice
- Pinch of salt
- 2 tbsp. frozen raspberries, optional

Directions:

1. In a non-stick saucepan add raspberries and let them simmer on medium heat for 10 minutes.
2. Add heavy cream to the raspberries; keep stirring until it comes to a boil.

3. In a large bowl whisk eggs and erythritol until the color changes to pale yellow and it gets fluffy.
4. Prepare a double boiler at home. Place the bowl with egg mixture on top and let the water get to a boil.
5. Add raspberry cream mixture, lemon juice to egg mixture in small batches and keep whisking. Stir for 5-7 minutes until it becomes thick.
6. Get if off the double boiler and let it cool down. Refrigerate it for 1 hour.
7. Add vodka and give it a mix. Place the bowl in the freezer and keep stirring after every 30 minutes for the next 2 hours.
8. Let it freeze for a total of 5-6 hours for best results.
9. Keep it at room temperature for 10 minutes. Top it with frozen raspberries.

White Chocolate Raspberry Ice Cream

Serves: 04

Ingredients:

- 3/4 cup frozen raspberries
- 2 egg yolks
- 1-1/2 tbsp. cocoa butter, roughly chopped
- 1-1/4 cup heavy whipped cream
- 1/2 cup almond milk, unsweetened
- 1/8 tsp. stevia extract
- 1 tsp. gelatin powder
- 1/2 tsp. vanilla extract
- 2 tbsp. vodka, optional
- 1/4 cup erythritol

Directions:

1. Freeze a metal pan overnight.

2. In a non-stick saucepan, mix cream, almond milk and sweeteners over medium heat. Stir until sweeteners are dissolved.
3. In a medium bowl, whisk egg yolks, vanilla extract and stevia. Slowly add 1 cup of cream mixture. Whisk continuously to temper the yolks so it doesn't scramble.
4. Add chopped cocoa butter once mixture is removed from the heat. Give it a minute to melt and combine.
5. Sprinkle xanthan gum over mixture and whisk continuously to combine.
6. Pour the mixture in an overnight frozen pan, let it cool for 15 minutes and cling wrap. Store the mixture to chill for 3 hours.
7. Mix vodka and transfer the mixture into an Ice cream machine to churn for 40 minutes.
8. Pour the mixture in an airtight container, mix frozen raspberries and freeze for 2 hours.
9. Keep the ice cream at room temperature 10 minutes before serving.

Avocado Ice Cream

Serves: 04

Ingredients:

- 2 ripe avocados
- 1/4 cup fresh mint leaves, loosely measured
- 1/4 cup basil leaves, loosely measured
- 1 cup full fat coconut milk, unsweetened
- 1/4 cup erythritol
- 1/2 tsp. fresh lemon juice
- 1 tbsp. + 1 tsp. MCT oil, unflavored

Directions:

1. Clean avocado by removing skin and seed. Cut into pieces.
2. In a blender/food processor mix all ingredients until smooth paste is formed.
3. Transfer mixture into a bowl and cover it with cling wrap. Chill in the fridge for 2 hours.
4. Add vodka and mix. Place it in the freezer for 4-5 hours.

5. Keep the ice cream at room temperature 10 minutes before serving.

Gingerbread Ice Cream

Serves: 04

Ingredients:

- 1/2 cup ginger, minced
- 1/2 cup almond milk, unsweetened
- 1 cup heavy whipping cream
- 2 egg yolks
- 1/2 tsp. vanilla extract
- 1/2 cup swerve sweetener
- 1 tsp. powdered erythritol
- 3/4 tsp. cinnamon, powdered
- 1 tsp. ground ginger
- 1/8 tsp. xanthan gum
- 1/4 tsp. clove, powdered
- 1 tbsp. vodka

Directions:

1. Freeze a metal pan overnight.

2. In a non-stick saucepan, mix almond milk, cream, minced ginger over medium heat. Let it simmer and remove it from the heat. Let it sit covered for 30 minutes.
3. On medium heat add sweetener to the cream mixture and stir until dissolved.
4. In a bowl, add erythritol, cinnamon, clove, ground ginger and whisk. Add half of the hot cream mixture and whisk continuously.
5. Once combined, pour the mixture to the balance cream in the saucepan. On medium stir continuously for 5-7 minutes.
6. Transfer the mixture into the overnight frozen pan and allow it to cool for 15 minutes. Wrap mixture with cling wrap and store it in the fridge for 2-3 hours.
7. Once chilled, mix in vodka and vanilla extract.
8. Sprinkle xanthan gum and whisk vigorously.
9. Transfer it in an airtight container and freeze the same for 4-5 hours.
10. Stir after every 30 mins for initial 2 hours.
11. Keep the ice cream at room temperature 10 minutes before serving.

Peach Ice Cream

Serves: 04

Ingredients:

- 1-1/2 peaches
- 3/4 cup heavy whipping cream
- 1/4 cup almond milk, unsweetened
- 2-1/2 tbsp. xylitol
- Pinch of salt
- 1/2 tbsp. fresh lemon juice
- 2 egg yolks
- 1/2 tsp. vanilla extract
- 3 tbsp. erythritol
- 1/4 tsp. xanthan gum
- 1 tbsp. vodka

Directions:

1. Place a medium pan/container in the freezer at the start of the process.

2. Slice peaches in a medium bowl; mix it with xylitol and lemon juice. Let it sit for 30 minutes until peaches start to release its juice. Mash it well with a fork.
3. Combine almond milk, cream and erythritol in a saucepan over low heat. Stir frequently and let it simmer.
4. In a large bowl whisk egg yolks and salt until the color changes to pale yellow and smooth. Slowly pour 1/2 cup egg yolk to cream mixture and whisk continuously.
5. Now pour egg -cream mixture into the saucepan and mix it with the remaining cream. Stir frequently, let it cook until it gets thick and starts to stick to the back of the spoon.
6. Quickly pour the mixture into the chilled pan from the freezer. Let it cool for about 10 minutes. Add xylitol and mix in the mashed peaches, whisk once to combine.
7. Place the mixture in the fridge for 3-4 hours.
8. Mix vodka, transfer it in an airtight container and freeze the same for 4-5 hours.
9. Stir after every 30 mins for an initial 2 hours.
10. Keep the ice cream at room temperature 10 minutes before serving.

Pina Colada Ice Cream

Serves: 04

Ingredients:

- 2 tbsp. pineapple extract.
- 2 egg yolks
- 1/2 cup full fat coconut milk, unsweetened
- 3/4 cup heavy whipping cream
- 1/4 cup erythritol
- 1 tbsp white rum
- Pinch of salt

Directions:

1. In a large bowl, whisk heavy cream until it forms soft peaks and becomes fluffy.
2. Combine coconut milk, egg yolk, pineapple extract, erythritol, white rum and pinch of salt in a food processor/blender and make a smooth paste.
3. Fold in mixture into cream until completely combined.

4. Place the mixture in the fridge for 3-4 hours.
5. Mix vodka, transfer it in an airtight container and freeze the same for 4-5 hours.
6. Stir after every 30 mins for initial 2 hours and serve.

Black Sesame Ice Cream

Serves: 04

Ingredients:

Black sesame paste
- 2 drops stevia
- 1-1/2 tbsp. chia seeds
- 1-1/2 tbsp. black sesame seeds
- 1/2 cup almond milk, unsweetened

Ice cream
- 3 tbsp. keto friendly maple syrup
- 3 tbsp. black sesame paste
- 1/4 cup, full fat coconut milk, unsweetened and chilled overnight
- 3/4 cup heavy whipping cream
- 1/2 tsp. vanilla extract
- Pinch of salt
- Pinch of active charcoal powder, optional
- Strawberry compote, optional

Strawberry compote
- 1/2 cup fresh strawberries
- 2 tbsp. fresh orange juice
- 1/2 tbsp. chia seeds
- 1/8 tsp. vanilla extract

Directions:

1. **Black sesame paste**: Grind chia seeds and black sesame seeds in a small grinder. Grind it to powder.
2. In a small bowl, add almond milk, stevia and mix ground chia and black sesame powder to it. Almond milk will get absorbed by chia seeds, stir it until you get a fine paste.
3. **Ice cream**: Separate the thick portion of coconut milk from the liquid and we will use only the thick part in this recipe.
4. In a blender/food processor blend chilled coconut milk, vanilla extract, maple syrup, charcoal powder, salt, black sesame paste, until it gives a creamy smooth texture. It could take up to 1 minute.
5. Transfer it to a metal bowl evenly and make a smooth surface.

6. Cover and store in the freezer for 3-4 hours.
7. Stir after every 15 mins until it becomes more solid.
8. **Strawberry compote**: Chop strawberries roughly, mix it in a pot along with orange juice, vanilla extract. Put the lid on and let it cook for about 15 minutes.
9. Let the orange juice reduce further for about 10 minutes.
10. Add chia seeds and transfer it to a jar, let it cool completely and it will start becoming thick.
11. Use the same as topping on the Ice cream.

Vanilla Cake Ice Cream

Serves: 05

Ingredients:

- 4 tbsp. keto collagen, chocolate flavor
- 1-3/4 cup heavy whipping cream
- 1/4 cup + 1 tbsp erythritol
- 2 egg yolks
- 3/4 cup full fat coconut milk, unsweetened
- 1 tsp. vanilla extract

Directions:

1. In a large saucepan, whisk heavy cream, coconut milk, vanilla extract, erythritol, and eggs. On medium heat, cook for 5 minutes.
2. Add keto collagen and stir. Keep it aside to cool.
3. Strain the mixture into a container and freeze for 4 hours.
4. Keep at room temperature 10 minutes before serving.

Fried Vanilla Ice Cream

Serves: 05

Ingredients:

Ice cream
- 1 vanilla bean preferably, if not 1 tbsp vanilla extract
- 3 eggs, separated
- 1/4 cup fresh lemon juice
- 1 cup heavy whipping cream
- 1/4 cup + 1 tbsp erythritol

Frying
- 1/2 cup keto breadcrumbs
- 3 eggs
- Sugar-free chocolate syrup or your choice of flavor for topping
- Oil for deep frying
- 1/8 cup erythritol

Directions:

1. Whisk egg whites and add lemon juice. Once it thickens, add powdered erythritol. Stop once stiff peaks are formed.
2. In another bowl, whisk heavy cream until soft. Do not over mix.
3. Mix egg yolks and vanilla bean in a small bowl.
4. Fold egg whites in cream mixture. Add egg yolk mixture and fold gently.
5. Pour the mixture in a metal container / pan and place it in the freezer for 2 hours.
6. After 2 hours, scoop ice cream and place each scoop separately on a tray. Freeze the tray for 20 minutes.
7. While that is happening, Beat 3 eggs in a bowl and place breadcrumbs in another flat dish.
8. Heat oil in a heavy skillet.
9. Remove scooped ice cream from the freezer and coat each scoop separately in first breadcrumbs, dip it in egg wash and again coat it with breadcrumbs.
10. Fry each scoop for 30-45 seconds until it turns golden brown.
11. Remove and Serve immediately, top it with chocolate sauce.

Brownie Ice Cream

Serves: 04

Ingredients:

- 1/2 tbsp. almond butter, no chunky/nutty
- 1/4 cup sugar-free dark chocolate chips
- 2 fudgy chocolate keto brownies
- 1 egg yolk, room temperature
- 1/4 tsp. vanilla extract
- 1 cup heavy whipping cream
- 2 tbsp. powdered monk fruit

Directions:

1. Recommended to freeze metal containers overnight or 6 hours before you start the process for good results.
2. In a saucepan, heat 1/2 cup heavy cream over low heat. Mix chocolate chips to the cream and stir continuously until fully melted. Allow to cool.

3. Beat egg yolks and monk fruit together until mixture turns pale yellow and thick.
4. Add egg mixture to chocolate mixture once cooled and combine. Heat the pan on low and stir continuously until it thickens. Do not let it boil.
5. Whip the remaining cream by hand mixer until stiff peaks are formed. Add almond butter with cooled chocolate mixture and fold.
6. Pour mixture in a chilled metal container and freeze for 2 hours, stir every 15 minutes.
7. Remove from the freezer and fold in brownie chunks, freeze for 2-3 hours.
8. Allow the Ice cream to sit at room temperature 10-15 minutes before your serve.

Maple Bacon Ice Cream

Serves: 04

Ingredients:

- 1 cup heavy cream
- 1 cup almond milk, unsweetened
- 2 large egg yolks
- Pinch of glycerin
- 1/8 tsp. salt
- 2 tbsp. + 2 tsp. erythritol
- 1/2 tbsp. maple syrup
- 1/4 tsp. vanilla extract
- 5 pork bacon slices

Directions:

1. In a large bowl, whisk together egg yolks, salt and xanthan gum. Set aside.
2. Heat almond milk and cream in a saucepan. Do not stir; it is done when bubbles are formed around the pan.
3. Slowly mix almond milk into egg yolks. Whisk continuously to avoid eggs from solidifying.

4. Meanwhile preheat the oven 400°F.
5. Add xylitol and transfer mixture to saucepan, cook on low heat until it starts to thicken. Keep stirring. It is done when the mixture starts to stick to the back of the spoon without running off.
6. Take it off heat, add maple syrup, vanilla extract, and glycerin and stir well.
7. Pour into the container and chill in the fridge for 30 minutes until completely cooled.
8. To cook bacon, line parchment paper over the tray or baking sheet. Place bacon strips on parchment paper and put the sheet in the preheated oven. Allow to bake for 20 minutes or until crisp depending on how your oven works.
9. Remove from the oven and place it on a paper towel to drain excess fat. Let it sit for 5 minutes. Crumble bacon strips into bits.
10. Once Ice cream batter has cooled, pour the mixture into Ice cream maker for 30 minutes or until it is thick. Add bacon bits and churn for another 5 minutes.
11. Eat it immediately as soft ice cream or freeze for 2 hours for a thick version.

Almond Milk Ice Cream

Serves: 04

Ingredients:

Ice cream
- 1-1/2 cup almond milk, unsweetened
- 3 large egg yolks
- 1/4 cup monkfruit sweetener
- Pinch of sea salt
- 1/2 tsp. vanilla extract

Choco-chip cookie dough
- 2 tbsp. monk fruit sweetener
- A quarter cup of almond flour
- 1/2 tsp. vanilla extract
- 3 tbsp. melted butter
- Pinch of sea salt
- 3 large egg yolks
- 1/8 cup sugar-free dark chocolate chips

Directions:

1. Recommended to freeze metal container overnight or 6 hours before you start the process for good results.
2. In a large bowl, whisk together egg yolks, monk fruit, sea salt until it turns pale yellow and thick. Set aside.
3. Heat almond milk until it starts to simmer.
4. Pour almond milk into egg yolk mixture slowly; whisk vigorously to avoid scrambling of eggs. Once the mixture is combined transfer it to a saucepan on low heat and stir frequently for 3-4 minutes.
5. Add vanilla extract and whisk until it is frothy. Transfer mixture to a container and refrigerate for 3-4 hours.
6. Meanwhile, for cookie dough beat together monk fruit and butter. Add in vanilla extract and blend again.
7. Add sea salt and almond flour, beat until cookie dough like consistency is formed. Mix chocolate chips in the mixture.
8. After 4 hours, pour Ice cream mixture into the container that is chilled overnight.
9. Let it freeze for 2 hours. Stir every 15 minutes until it starts to get thick.

10. Make a small pinch of cookie dough and add to the Ice cream after 2 hours and stir well.
11. Freeze it further for 1 hour and serve if you prefer soft Ice cream or freeze for 4 – 5 hours for a firmer Ice cream.

Fatty Coconut Cream Ice Cream

Serves: 05

Ingredients:

- 1-1/4 cup heavy whipping cream
- 1/2 cup shredded coconut, unsweetened
- 2 tbsp. MCT oil
- 2 egg yolks
- 3 tbsp. butter
- 1-1/2 tbsp. coconut oil
- 2 tbsp. vanilla extract
- 1/2 tsp. coconut extract, optional
- 4 -5 drops of liquid stevia
- Pinch of salt

Directions:

1. In a large bowl, whisk together egg yolks, stevia and sea salt until it turns pale yellow and thick. Set aside.

2. On low heat, add heavy cream to the saucepan and let it simmer.
3. Remove from heat; add coconut oil, butter, MCT oil, vanilla extract and coconut extract. Whisk well until combined.
4. Pour cream mixture into egg yolks and whisk constantly to avoid scrambling of eggs.
5. Once mixed, cook mixture on low heat until it gets thick. You will know the doneness once it starts to cover the back of a spoon. Take it off heat at this stage.
6. Add shredded coconut to this mixture and combine.
7. Let the mixture cool in the fridge for 3-4 hours.
8. Give it a good mix and transfer it in an airtight or metal container. Place it in the freezer for 5-6 hours.
9. Stir every 30 mins for the first 2 hours or until it gets thick.
10. Remove from the freezer 10 minutes before you want to serve.

Cookies and Cream Ice Cream

Serves: 06

Ingredients:

Cookie crumb

- 6 tbsp. almond flour
- 1 egg
- 1/8 cup erythritol
- 1/2 tsp. vanilla extract
- 1 tbsp. coconut oil, softened
- 1/8 cup cocoa powder
- 1/4 tsp. baking powder

Ice cream
- 1/4 cup almond milk, unsweetened
- 1/2 tbsp. vanilla extract
- 1-1/2 cup heavy whipping cream
- 1/4 cup erythritol

Directions:

1. **Cookie**: Preheat the oven to 300°F. Take a 9-inch pan and cover it with parchment paper.
2. In a medium bowl, sift cocoa powder, almond flour, salt, erythritol, and baking powder and mix until combined well. Add vanilla extract and coconut oil until batter turns into fine crumbs.
3. Add egg and blend with the help of a hand blender until it gets thick like a dough.
4. Transfer the dough on the pan and spread it evenly by spatula or hand.
5. Bake for 20 minutes. Remove from the pan and let cool.
6. Break the cookie into small crumbs only when it is completely cooled.
7. **Ice cream**: In another bowl, blend whipping cream with an electric mixer until stiff peaks form.
8. Add erythritol, vanilla extract and whisk until combined completely.
9. Mix almond milk to it and whisk again until it gets thick.
10. Pour mixture in an Ice cream maker and churn for 30 minutes until it gets to soft serve consistency.

11. Add the cookie crumbs to it and let it churn until evenly mixed.
12. Transfer the Ice cream to a metal container and freeze for 2-3 hours.

Saffron and Rosewater Persian Ice Cream

Serves: 04

Ingredients:

- 1 cup Half and half
- 1 cup heavy whipping cream
- 2 egg yolks
- Pinch of salt
- 1/2 tsp. vanilla extract
- 1/2 cup Monk Fruit sweetener
- 1/2 tsp. rose water
- 1/8 tsp. xanthan gum
- 1/8 tsp. saffron powder or 4-5 saffron strands
- 1/4 cup pistachio, coarsely chopped
- Dried roses, for garnish

Directions:

1. Boil 3 tbsp. water and add saffron strands in it. Remove from heat and let it sit for 20 minutes.

2. Take a large bowl and another bowl that could sit in it. Fill the large water with icy water and sit the medium bowl over it.
3. Beat egg yolks in another bowl until pale yellow and thick.
4. In a saucepan on low heat, whisk half and half with heavy cream, monk fruit sweetener, salt. Remove saffron strands from water and pour the saffron water into this mixture. Whisk again until all combined.
5. Slowly pour about 1/4 cup of hot cream mixture to beaten eggs for tempering and whisk vigorously. Pour the mixture back into the saucepan and keep stirring frequently on low heat. Once it sticks to the back of a spoon, turn off the heat. Do not let it boil.
6. Let the mixture cool and add vanilla extract and rose water to it. Sprinkle xanthan gum and whisk continuously.
7. Transfer mixture into the metal container and freeze for 4-6 hours.
8. Stir the mixture every 30 minutes for initial 2 hours. Add chopped pistachio after stirring the last time and mix well until combined. Continue freezing.
9. Garnish with dried rose petals before serving.

Cereal Ice Cream

Serves: 04

Ingredients:

- 1 cup keto friendly coconut almond cereals, crushed
- 1-1/2 cup heavy whipping cream
- 1/4 cup almond milk, unsweetened
- 1/2 tbsp. vanilla extract
- 1/4 cup erythritol
- 3 tbsp. roasted almonds, chopped

Directions:

1. In a medium bowl, blend whipping cream with an electric mixer until stiff peaks form.
2. Add erythritol, vanilla extract and whisk until combined completely.
3. Mix almond milk to it and whisk again until it gets thick.
4. Pour mixture in a metal container and freeze for 2 hours.
5. Remove Ice cream from the container and blend it.

6. Add crushed cereals and chopped almonds to the Ice cream. Transfer it back to the metal container and freeze for another 2 hours.

Peanut Butter and Jelly Ice Cream

Serves: 04

Ingredients:

- 1/2 cup Keto friendly peanut butter
- 1/4 cup Keto friendly Jelly
- 1 cup heavy whipping cream
- 1/4 cup coconut milk, unsweetened
- 1/2 tbsp. vanilla extract
- 1/4 cup erythritol

Directions:

1. In a small bowl, add peanut butter, 1 tbsp. coconut milk, and 1 tbsp erythritol and stir well until combined well.
2. In another bowl, blend whipping cream with an electric mixer until stiff peaks form.
3. Add remaining erythritol, vanilla extract, and coconut milk and whisk until it thickens.

4. Pour mixture in an Ice cream maker, churn for 30 minutes. Add peanut butter sauce and churn for another minute.
5. Transfer Ice cream to a metal container. Make zig zag lines with the help of butter knife and add jelly in those zig zag lines. Swirl the Ice cream and freeze for 2 hours.

S'mores Ice Cream

Serves: 04

Ingredients:

- 1 cup Keto mini marshmallows or chopped in smaller pieces
- 1/2 cup Keto friendly graham crackers, crumbled
- 3 tbsp. cocoa powder
- 1-1/4 cup heavy cream
- 1 tsp. vanilla extract
- 1/2 cup sugar free dark chocolate
- Pinch of salt
- 1/4 cup erythritol
- 1 tbsp. vodka or gin, optional

Directions:

1. Keep a freezer friendly container overnight in the freezer, preferably metal.

2. In a saucepan, melt dark chocolate on low heat and let it cool.
3. Whisk heavy cream, erythritol, and vanilla extract in the chilled bowl until it is soft and fluffy.
4. Add melted chocolate, cocoa powder, pinch of salt, vodka and combine.
5. Pour mixture in a metal pan / airtight container and freeze for 5-6 hours.
6. Stir the mixture every 30 minutes for the first 2 hours.
7. Add Marshmallows and graham crackers to the Ice cream after 2 hours and stir it well. Continue freezing.
8. Remove Ice cream 15 minutes and let it sit at room temperature before serving.

Strawberry Rhubarb Ice Cream

Serves: 04

Ingredients:

Strawberry Rhubarb Sauce
- 1/4 cup strawberries, sliced
- 1/4 cup rhubarb, diced
- 1 tbsp. granulated stevia
- 1/2 tsp. fresh lemon juice
- 1 tsp. water
- 1/4 tsp. xanthan gum

Ice cream
- 1-1/2 cup heavy cream
- 1/4 cup granulated stevia
- 1/4 tsp. vanilla extract
- 1/2 cup almond milk, unsweetened

Directions:

1. **Strawberry and rhubarb sauce**: add stevia and xanthan gum in a saucepan. Add water and lemon juice gradually and whisk until combined.
2. Add rhubarb and strawberries, place the pan on medium heat and stir frequently.
3. Let it cook until rhubarb and strawberries soften, it would take 5-7 minutes then remove from heat. Set it aside to cool.
4. **Ice cream**: In a large bowl, add heavy cream, stevia and vanilla extract, whisk with an electric mixer until stiff peaks form.
5. Add almond milk in 2 or 3 batches and blend every time a new batch is poured into the cream. Whisk until it thickens.
6. Transfer to an ice cream machine and churn for 30 minutes or as per manufacturer's instructions.
7. Once it reaches the consistency of soft ice cream and gets a smooth texture, transfer it to a container. Add strawberry rhubarb sauce and swirl with butter knife.

8. Freeze for 3-4 hours. Stir every 30 minutes for the first 2 hours.

Chocolate Banana Walnut Ice Cream

Serves: 04

Ingredients:

- 1/4 cup walnuts, chopped
- 1 cup heavy whipping cream
- 1/2 cup almond milk, unsweetened
- 6 tbsp. monk fruit sweetener
- 1 tbsp. gelatin
- 2 tbsp. IMO syrup
- 1 large egg
- 2 tbsp. keto friendly dark chocolate, chopped
- 1/4 tsp. Banana flavoring
- 1/2 tsp. vanilla extract

Directions:

1. Mix sweetener and gelatin in a large saucepan and whisk. Add egg and almond milk, on low heat whisk continuously until it starts to simmer.

2. Once it simmers, place the pan in an ice bath and let cool.
3. Once it comes to room temperature, whisk whipping cream, IMO syrup, banana flavoring and vanilla extract.
4. Pour mixture in a container and freeze for 2 hours. Stir after every 30 minutes.
5. Add chopped walnuts and chopped chocolate pieces and give it a good mix.
6. Freeze for further 3-4 hours.

Cream Cannoli Ice Cream

Serves: 05

Ingredients:

- 1 tsp. ground cinnamon
- 2/3 cup heavy whipping cream
- 1-1/4 cup ricotta, whole milk
- 1/3 cup + 1 tbsp. powdered erythritol
- 1 tbsp. keto-friendly chocolate chips

Directions:

1. Place ricotta cheese into muslin cloth or cheesecloth. Squeeze excess water from cheese and transfer the dry cheese into a dry bowl.
2. Add vanilla extract, cinnamon, sweetener and combine. Set aside.
3. In a small bowl, whip heavy cream until stiff peaks form. Fold cream into ricotta cheese.
4. Fold in chocolate chips and freeze for 2-3 hours.

Snicker Ice Cream

Serves: 04

Ingredients:

Bottom layer
- 8 drops liquid stevia
- 1-1/2 tbsp. peanut butter
- 1-1/2 tbsp. protein powder, no flavor
- 2 tbsp. full fat milk, coconut or almond or heavy cream

Middle layer
- 1 tbsp. maple syrup
- 1-1/2 tbsp. butter
- 1-1/2 tbsp. peanut butter
- 1 tbsp. crushed peanuts, optional but recommended

Top layer
- 1-1/2 tbsp. butter
- 2 tbsp. chocolate, unsweetened
- 8 drops liquid stevia

Directions:

1. Recommend using a container with a flat base for this recipe.
2. **Bottom layer**: In a medium bowl, add milk, peanut butter, protein powder, stevia and whisk until smooth.
3. Pour mixture into a flat base container and place in the freezer.
4. **Middle layer**: In a small saucepan on low heat, mix butter, peanut butter until combined. Take off heat, add maple syrup and combine. Set aside.
5. **Top layer**: In the same saucepan on low heat, add butter and chocolate, mix it until well combined. Add stevia and combine. Set aside.
6. Remove the bottom layer from the freezer, add caramel layer and sprinkle crushed peanuts. Pour chocolate layer and spread it evenly.
7. Freeze for 2-3 hours.
8. Instead of scooping, cut it with a knife and serve.

Cranberry and Rum Ice Cream

Serves: 04

Ingredients:

- 1 cup dried cranberries
- 1/2 cup almond milk, unsweetened
- 1 cup heavy cream
- 1/4 cup maple syrup
- 1/4 cup rum
- 3 egg yolks
- 1/2 tsp. vanilla extract

Directions:

1. In a small bowl, add rum and dried cranberries. Cover and keep aside for 3-4 hours.
2. In a saucepan, add the rum and soaked cranberries and let the alcohol evaporate on low heat. Make sure cranberries do not dry up and there should be some liquid left for cranberries to be moist.

3. Combine heavy cream, almond milk, maple syrup on a saucepan and let it simmer on low heat.
4. Whisk egg yolks in a separate bowl until frothy.
5. Pour half of the cream mixture on the egg yolks to temper, whisk continuously. Pour the egg mixture back on the saucepan and bring it to a simmer. Turn the heat off when the mixture starts to thicken. Whisk continuously.
6. Meanwhile, prepare a large bowl with ice. Transfer mixture into a medium bowl and place the bowl on the larger bowl for ice bath. Let it cool.
7. Freeze for 2 hours. Stir every 30 minutes and after 2 hours add rum and cranberries into the Ice cream and mix well.
8. Freeze for further 2 hours and serve.

Orange and Dark Chocolate Ice Cream

Serves: 04

Ingredients:

- 2 tbsp. Orange zest, grated
- 1/2 cup dark chocolate chips, unsweetened
- 3 tbsp. cocoa powder
- 1-1/4 cup heavy cream
- 1 tsp. vanilla extract
- 1/2 cup sugar free dark chocolate
- Pinch of salt
- 1/4 cup erythritol
- 1 tbsp. vodka or gin, optional

Directions:

1. Keep a freezer friendly container overnight in the freezer, preferably metal.
2. In a saucepan, melt dark chocolate on low heat and let it cool.

3. Whisk heavy cream, erythritol, and vanilla extract in the chilled bowl until it is soft and fluffy.
4. Add melted chocolate, cocoa powder, pinch of salt, vodka and combine.
5. Pour mixture in a metal pan / airtight container and freeze for 5-6 hours.
6. Stir the mixture every 30 minutes for the first 2 hours.
7. Add orange zest and dark chocolate chips into the Ice cream and mix well. Continue freezing.

Cherry Kefir Ice Cream

Serves: 04

Ingredients:

- 1-1/2 cup double fermented, keto friendly Kefir
- 1 tsp. vanilla extract
- 1 cup cherries, pitted
- 1/2 cup erythritol
- Pinch of salt
- 1 tbsp. vodka or gin, optional

Directions:

1. In a blender, add Kefir, cherries, erythritol, salt and vanilla extract. Blend until smooth.
2. Add vodka and combine.
3. Pour mixture in a metal pan/airtight container and freeze for 4-5 hours.
4. Stir the mixture every 30 minutes for the first 2 hours.

Red Velvet Ice Cream Cake

Serves: 08

Ingredients:

Red velvet cake

- 3/4 cup of almond flour
- Quarter cup of coconut flour
- 1/4 cup baking chocolate
- 3 eggs
- 3/4 cup unsalted butter
- 1 tablespoon baking powder
- 1 cup granulated erythritol or any other sweetener
- 1 tbsp. red food color
- 1 tsp. white vinegar
- Pinch of sea salt

Ice Cream Layer

- 1/2 cup cream cheese, chilled

- 1 cup heavy cream
- 1/2 cup granulated erythritol or any other sweetener
- 1/2 tsp. vanilla extract
- Pinch of sea salt

Chocolate shell

- 1-1/2 tbsp. keto friendly dark cocoa powder
- 1-1/2 tbsp. granulated erythritol or any other sweetener
- 1-1/2 tbsp. coconut oil, melted

Red Vanilla topping

- 1/2 tbsp. heavy cream
- 1-1/2 tbsp. coconut oil, melted
- 1/2 tsp. vanilla extract
- 1/2 tsp. red dye

Directions:

1. Preheat the oven to 350°F. Grease a 9-inch pan and keep it ready.

2. Prepare a double boiler on low heat, place baking chocolate and let it melt. Set aside.
3. Sift coconut flour, almond flour, salt and baking soda in a large bowl and set aside.
4. In another bowl, whisk butter, sweetener, red food color and melted chocolate with the help of an electric mixer.
5. Add one egg at a time to the butter and sweetener mixture and whisk after adding each egg until well incorporated. Stir in white vinegar.
6. Add flour mixture to the wet mixture and combine well with an electric mixture.
7. Add mixture to the greased pan and bake for 30 minutes or until the inserted toothpick is clean. Let it cool.
8. Once cooled, crumble cake and divide in two parts. One part will be the base of the Ice cream and another will be served as topping.
9. In a pan around preferably square, add half crumbs and press them with a spoon.
10. With an electric blender, whisk cream cheese, sea salt, vanilla extract, sweetener and mix at high speed. Add cold whipping cream to the mixture and whisk until fully incorporated.

11. Transfer the mixture on top of the bottom layer of cake crumbs and spread gently and evenly. Cover with cling wrap and freeze for 4 hours.
12. Meanwhile for chocolate shell add melted coconut oil, sweetener, cocoa powder in a small bowl and combine.
13. For red vanilla topping, add sweetener, whipping cream in a small saucepan and heat. Once heated red color and vanilla extract, mix well.
14. Once ice cream is chilled, remove from the freezer. If sauces have thickened, heat them again and pour on the chilled ice cream immediately. You will see it start to harden almost immediately after it is poured.
15. Serve immediately or freeze again and eat as per convenience.

Brown Butter Bourbon Pecan Ice Cream

Serves: 05

Ingredients:
- 1-1/4 cup heavy cream
- 1-1/2 cup half and half
- 1/4 cup + 1 tsp. butter
- 2 tbsp. toffee syrup, sugar-free
- 4 egg yolks
- 1/4 cup + 1 tsp. granulated stevia
- 1 tsp. vanilla extract
- Pinch of salt
- 1/4 tsp. xanthan gum
- 1/4 cup Toasted pecans, chopped
- 2-1/2 tbsp. bourbon

Directions:

1. In a heavy saucepan, melt butter on low heat until it turns golden brown. Do not let it get too dark.

2. In the same saucepan, add heavy cream, sweetener, half and half, salt and let it cook on low heat. Do not let it boil, keep stirring and remove from heat once bubbles start forming around the edge.
3. Beat eggs in a small bowl until fluffy. Pour half of the heavy cream mixture into eggs gradually and keep stirring continuously to avoid eggs from scrambling.
4. Pour the egg mixture back into the saucepan and let it cook until it thickens. Remove from heat once it starts to stick to the back of a spoon.
5. Transfer mixture into bowl, cover and refrigerate for 5-6 hours or even overnight.
6. Once cooled, add bourbon, vanilla extract, xanthan gum, and toffee syrup and whisk vigorously.
7. Freeze for 4 hours; stir every 30 minutes for an initial two hours. Add roasted chopped pecans after 2 hours. Mix well and continue to freeze.

Orange and Black Licorice Ice Cream

Serves: 05

Ingredients:

Orange base

- 4 large egg yolks
- 1/2 cup erythritol or choice of sweetener
- Pinch of salt
- 1 cup heavy cream
- 1 cup almond milk, unsweetened
- 2 tsp. blood orange extract
- Orange food coloring

Licorice Ribbon

- 2 tbsp. water
- 1/2 cup erythritol or choice of sweetener
- 1/4 cup butter
- 1/4 cup almond milk, unsweetened

- 1-1/2 tsp. anise extract
- Black food color

Directions:

1. **Orange base**: Beat egg yolks with salt and sweetener until they turn pale yellow and fluffy. Add almond milk gradually and whisk each time after adding milk.
2. Add heavy cream and whisk until totally combined.
3. Heat until it starts to boil, whisk continuously. Remove from heat; add orange extract and food color. Mix well and set aside to cool.
4. **Licorice base**: Boil sweetener and water together in a bowl. Let it simmer, turn off once it starts to boil and changes color to golden.
5. Add butter and whisk continuously, it may splutter. Mix until melted completely.
6. Mix anise extract and almond milk, stir to combine. Add black food color. Allow mixture to cool completely.
7. Once both mixtures come to room temperature, refrigerate them for 4 hours.

8. Now freeze mixtures separately in the freezer for 2 hours. Stir every 30 minutes until it thickens. In a large container, add scoops of orange and black ice cream randomly so both colors can be mixed.
9. Press it down with help of spatula and spread evenly.
10. Freeze for 3-4 hours and serve.

Maple Habanero Ice Cream

Serves: 06

Ingredients:
- 1 cup maple syrup
- 1 cup almond milk, unsweetened
- 1 cup heavy cream
- 5 habaneros
- 1/2 cup protein powder, vanilla flavor
- 1/2 tsp. vanilla extract
- 1/8 tsp. xanthan gum

Directions:

1. Cut and remove all seeds from habaneros.
2. In a heavy saucepan, heat heavy cream, maple syrup, almond milk and salt.
3. Let it simmer and remove from heat. Whisk in protein powder, xanthan gum, and vanilla extract and mix well. Stir in habaneros. Place in the fridge, let it steep overnight.
4. Strain habaneros and freeze the mixture for 2 hours.

Green Chili and Mint Ice Cream

Serves: 04

Ingredients:

- 1/2 cup coconut milk, unsweetened
- 1 cup heavy cream
- 1 tsp. vodka, optional
- 1/2 cup cream cheese
- 2 fresh green chilies
- Handful mint leaves
- 1/2 tsp. vanilla extract
- 1/2 tsp. fresh lemon juice
- Pinch of sea salt
- 2 tbsp. erythritol

Directions:

1. Cut and chop green chilies and mint leaves into fine pieces.

2. Blend cream cheese and coconut milk on high speed until well mixed.
3. Add vanilla extract, lemon juice, salt, whipping cream and whisk again until combined.
4. Add erythritol and blend again.
5. Now add chopped chilies and mint leaves and blend for a minute.
6. Add vodka and mix.
7. Pour mixture into freezer friendly container and freeze for 4 hours.
8. Stir every 30 minutes for initial 2 hours and continue freezing.

Cauliflower Ice Cream

Serves: 05

Ingredients:
- 3/4 cup cauliflower florets
- 1/2 cup coconut milk, unsweetened
- 1/8 cup coconut oil
- 1 tbsp. vanilla extract
- 1/4 cup maple syrup
- 1 tbsp. almond extract
- 1/2 cup cashews, soaked for 3-4 hours in warm water
- 1/4 cup chopped pistachios, for garnishing
- Pinch of sea salt

Directions:

1. Boil the cut cauliflowers until tender. Drain and let cool.
2. In a blender, add cauliflower, coconut milk, coconut oil, vanilla extract, almond extract, maple syrup, cashews and salt. Blend until combined.
3. Pour mixture into freezer friendly container and freeze.

4. Remove from the freezer after 2 hours and blend again. Pour mixture in a container and freeze for 2 more hours.

Garlic Ice Cream

Serves: 04

Ingredients:

- 2 garlic cloves, chopped
- 1/2 cup heavy cream
- 1/2 cup granulated erythritol
- 4 large egg yolks
- 1 cup almond milk, unsweetened
- 1 tbsp. vanilla extract
- Pinch of sea salt

Directions:

1. Freeze metal containers overnight.
2. In a saucepan, boil chopped garlic, almond milk and vanilla extract on medium heat. Remove immediately once it starts to boil.
3. Whisk erythritol, egg yolks and heavy cream in a medium bowl until combined.

4. Strain half of boiled garlic milk mixture into egg mixture, whisk continuously.
5. Return mixture to saucepan and cook over low heat until it thickens. Do not boil.
6. Pour mixture into a chilled metal container.
7. Freeze for 3-4 hours and serve.

Wasabi and Cucumber Ice Cream

Serves: 04

Ingredients:

- 2 tbsp. erythritol
- 1 cup full fat coconut milk, unsweetened
- 1 medium cucumber
- 1/2 fresh lemon juice
- 1 tbsp. wasabi paste
- Pinch of sea salt

Directions:

1. Peel and chop cucumber.
2. Add chopped cucumber, wasabi paste, sweetener, lemon juice and coconut milk to a blender and mix until smooth.
3. Pour mixer to freezer safe container and freeze for 6-8 hours.

4. Stir ice cream every hour to ensure air is incorporated. Repeat 2-3 times or until mixture is almost firm and continue freezing.

Black Charcoal Ice Cream

Serves: 04

Ingredients:

- 2-1/2 cups heavy whipping cream
- 1/4 cup confectioners erythritol
- 1 tsp. vanilla extract
- 1/4 cup almond milk, unsweetened
- 3 egg yolks
- 1-1/2 tbsp. activated charcoal
- 1 tsp. anise oil
- Pinch of sea salt

Directions:

1. Whisk almond milk, sea salt, egg yolks, erythritol and charcoal until smooth.
2. Place it in the fridge for 2 hours.
3. In a large bowl, whisk heavy cream until soft peaks form. Add anise oil and whisk again.

4. Remove mixture from the fridge. Fold heavy cream mixture into chilled egg mixture and transfer it to a freezer friendly pan.
5. Freeze for 3-4 hours and serve.

Dark Cherry and Chocolate Chunk Ice Cream

Serves: 04

Ingredients:

- 1/2 cup dark red cherries, pitted
- 1 cup heavy whipping cream
- 1/2 cup full fat almond milk, unsweetened
- 1/4 cup keto friendly dark chocolate, cut into chunks
- 1 large egg
- 1/4 cup erythritol
- Pinch of sea salt

Directions:

1. Refrigerate cherries and chocolate.
2. In a medium bowl, whisk eggs until they turn pale yellow and fluffy.
3. Add sugar in small portions and whisk each time after adding until it comes together.

4. Pour heavy cream and almond milk into it and blend again.
5. Transfer to a freezer friendly container and freeze for 4-5 hours.
6. After 2 hours, stir the mixture and add cherries and chocolate chunks to it. Mix well and continue freezing.

Amarenata Cherry Ice Cream

Serves: 04

Ingredients:

Ice Cream

- 1/2 cup coconut milk
- 1/4 cup erythritol, powdered
- 1-3/4 heavy whipping cream
- 2 egg yolks
- 1/4 cup low-carb Amarenata
- 6-7 drops liquid stevia extract
- 1 tsp. gelatin powder
- 1/2 tsp. vanilla extract

Low-carb Amarenata

- 3/4 cup frozen cherries or fresh cherries, pitted
- 1/2 tsp. ground cinnamon powder
- 1/2 tbsp. vanilla extract

- 1 tbsp. chia seeds, optional
- 1/4 cup erythritol
- 1/2 cup water

Directions:

1. **Low-carb Amarenata**: Add pitted cherries or frozen cherries in a non-stick pot. Add erythritol, water, cinnamon powder and vanilla extract.
2. Mix well, place it on low- medium heat and let it cook. Keep stirring frequently until mixture thickens. This may take up to 30 minutes.
3. Blend chia seeds in a grinder. Once mixture thickens, sprinkle chia seed powder and mix well. Cook for 5-7 minutes.
4. Let it sit for 20 minutes and refrigerate. Sauce will further thicken once it is cold.
5. **Ice cream**: In a saucepan, add 1 cup whipping cream, erythritol and stevia. Cook until it starts to simmer.
6. Whisk egg yolks with remaining 3/4 cup heavy cream. Pour 1/2 quantity of hot whipping cream mixture to egg

yolks and whisk continuously. Return this mixture to the saucepan and let it cook on low heat.
7. Mix gelatin with water and add it to the mixture.
8. Combine and set the pan over another large bowl filled with ice.
9. Let it cool completely. Add vanilla extract and 1/2 cup coconut milk to the mixture and mix well until combined.
10. Pour mixture into freezer friendly or an airtight container. Freeze for 6 hours.
11. Stir every 30 minutes for an initial 2 hours. Add the Amarenata over ice cream and mix a bit to create swirls.
12. Continue freezing.

Lavender Wild Berry Ice Cream

Serves: 04

Ingredients:
- 3/4 cup heavy cream
- 1 cup full fat almond milk/coconut milk, unsweetened
- 1/8 tsp. orange extract
- 1/2 cup wild blueberries
- 1/4 cup cream cheese, room temperature
- 1/8 cup water
- 1/4 cup + 1 tbsp. granulated erythritol
- 1/8 cup xanthan gum
- 1 small drop lavender essential oil, optional
- Pinch of sea salt

Directions:

1. In a saucepan, boil water with blueberries, 1 tbsp. erythritol. Let it simmer for 5-7 minutes and let it cool to become compote.

2. Mix 1 tbsp. milk with cream cheese, xanthan gum and salt in a small bowl and combine.
3. In a large pot, heat remaining milk, heavy cream and erythritol until it starts to boil. On low heat continue to boil for 3-4 minutes.
4. Once removed from heat, add cream cheese mixture.
5. Add blueberry compote and mix.
6. Refrigerate mixture for 4-6 hours.
7. Once chilled give it a stir and pour mixture into freezer friendly container. Cover and freeze for 3-4 hours.
8. Keep Ice cream at room temperature for 15 minutes before serving.

Cheddar Cheese Ice Cream

Serves: 04

Ingredients:

- 1 cup heavy cream
- 1/4 cup erythritol
- 1/2 cup mild cheddar cheese
- 3 large egg yolks

Directions:

1. Keep a freezer friendly container overnight in the freezer, preferably metal.
2. In a saucepan, warm heavy cream and erythritol.
3. Grate cheddar cheese in a bowl and set aside.
4. Whisk egg yolks in a separate bowl. Pour warm heavy cream mixture to temper eggs and whisk continuously. Return this mixture back to the saucepan and keep stirring over medium heat. Keep stirring until mixture starts to

become thick and stick to the back of the spatula. Do not boil.
5. Strain egg and cream mixture over grated cheese. Stir continuously until cheese is melted completely.
6. Place mixture in the fridge for 4-5 hours.
7. Remove and stir well, pour in a freezer friendly/airtight container. Freeze for 4 hours.
8. Stir every 15 minutes until ice cream starts to thicken, continue freezing.

Guava and Cream Cheese Ice Cream

Serves: 05

Ingredients:

- 1/2 cup heavy cream, chilled
- 1/2 cup keto friendly sour cream, chilled
- 1/2 cup cream cheese, room temperature and softened
- 1/2 cup erythritol granulated
- 1 tbsp. lemon juice
- 1/4 cup guava paste
- 1/2 cup water
- 1/2 tsp. guava extract
- 1/2 tsp. vanilla extract
- Pinch of sea salt

Directions:

1. In a bowl, whisk cream cheese until smooth. Add erythritol in 2-3 batches, beat mixture every time after adding

erythritol. Add heavy cream, sour cream, lemon juice, salt and vanilla extract. Whisk until well incorporated.
2. Cover bowl with cling wrap and store in the fridge for 2 hours until it is very cold.
3. In a skillet, cook guava paste with water over low-medium heat until melted completely. Keep mashing with a potato masher or fork. This may take 5-7 minutes.
4. After 2 hours, whisk cream cheese mixture and pour into a freezer friendly/airtight container. Freeze for 4 hours.
5. Stir every 15 minutes until ice cream starts to thicken. After 2 hours add guava paste into Ice cream and mix well. Continue freezing.

Conclusion

I want to thank you once again for choosing this book! I hope you enjoyed trying out the recipes as much as I did creating them!

Following a diet has never been this simple or delicious! If the thought of a diet conjures images of tasteless, bland, and boring food, it is time to change all this! The keto diet is all about eating to your heart's content, provided you follow a simple low-carb and high-fat eating protocol. You no longer have to compromise on your taste buds for the sake of your health. The keto diet is simple to follow and is sustainable in the long run. Unlike other fad diets, it isn't restrictive and includes a variety of ingredients.

Were there instances when you stopped yourself from eating your favorite foods for the sake of a diet? Do you want to eat foods you enjoy without any associated guilt? If yes, the recipes given in this book are perfect! There are various recipes given in this book, and explore them depending on what appeals to you. There is plenty to try from pumpkin spiced pecan pie ice cream, chocolate espresso sorbet, and peanut butter ice cream to strawberry ice cream and Nutella ice cream. Making ice creams is not a time-consuming process, provided you have the right recipe and ingredients on hand.

All the recipes given in this book are incredibly easy to understand and simple to follow. They are curated, keeping in mind the special requirements of the keto diet. So, the ingredients don't include any grains, unhealthy and artificial sugars, or unhealthy oils. Instead, they are filled with nourishing goodness packed into flavorful recipes. Also, you need not splurge on expensive ingredients. What more? You can whip up delicious and nutritious ice creams within no time like a pro! All you need to do is stock your pantry with keto-friendly ingredients required for the recipes given in this book. Select a recipe that strikes your fancy, follow the instructions, and voila!

Once you get the hang of it, you can experiment with different flavor combinations and see for yourself. Making ice creams is not rocket science. The key to your overall health and fitness lies in your hands. All you need to do is take the first step and get started! With the recipes in this book, you are essentially eating your way to a better and healthier you! So, what are you waiting for?

Thank you and all the best!

www.ingramcontent.com/pod-product-compliance
Lightning Source LLC
Chambersburg PA
CBHW071624080526
44588CB00010B/1259